A BOOK OF VERSE

By

THOMAS LOVE PEACOCK

British Library Cataloguing-in-Publication Data
A catalogue record for this book is available
from the British Library

CONTENTS

3

THOMAS LOVE PEACOCK

By Sir Walter Raleigh
from
On Writers and Writing

THERE is nothing misanthropical about Peacock. He admires, and loves. All that is simple and matter of affection, and private, is dear to him. He laughs at idealists, and makers of systems. Yet---here is the strange thing---he is not common sense against the idea. He has, deep down in him, a great love for ideas. How easy to make fun of Rousseau, Mme de Genlis, Thomas Day--- all that world of theory which belongs to the French Revolution! Peacock does make fun of it, but he has been touched by it. The two most virtuous characters in *Melincourt* are Sir Oran Haut-ton and Sylvan Forester---separate embodiments of the natural man of the revolutionary philosophy. Life in the woods---life in a cottage with a garden---Peacock is almost passionate about these. Yet he praises them chiefly in conversations that take place round tables amply suppled with old silver and madeira.

He was a friend of Shelley, and a wine-drinker---perhaps that best describes him. His friendship for Shelley had in it some kinship of ideas, not a merely personal liking. Indeed, Peacock himself was something of a theorist. He loved the consistency of the Latin mind; he adored logic; he loved a rebel, if the rebel was in earnest, as Shelley was. His ridicule of the other poets of the time turns for the most part on a single point, that they have given up their youthful creeds and have settled down in comfort.

Talk gives the structure of his books. They are a world of

talk. "It's all very fine talking," people say, "but is it practical?" In Peacock the standard is reversed. "It's all very practical, but is it fine talking?" The atmosphere of conviviality in the novels keeps the differences from bursting into drama. When the dispute waxes hot someone says, "Buz the bottle."

Allow for the difference between a persecuted preacher of the gospel and a prosperous clerk in the Examiner's office of the East India Company, and Peacock's work is a kindly *Pilgrim's Progress.* He gives his characters the same kind of names. Bunyan would have said it was a Pilgrm's Progress by Mr Byends of the City of Fairspeech.

Type in Peacock hardly ever passes into character. His work continually borders on character drawing, but he values the play of wit and theory too well. The whole world is a *salon* to him.

If there are any of Peacock's persons who are felt to be living human characters, they are to be found among his young ladies and his drunkards. The first are real, perhaps because they are pleasant and sensible (which few of the men are), perhaps because the author takes fewer freedoms in the portraiture. It is difficult to say exactly how they make so pleasant an impression---probably by their freedom from censoriousness, and by the good will of the other characters towards them. A novelist may learn something from the wisdom of Lord Halifax in his *Advice to a Daughter:*

"The triumph of wit is to make your good nature subdue your censure, to be quick in seeing fults and slow in exposing them. You are to consider that the invisible thing called a *Good Name* is made up of the breth of numbers that speak well of you; so that if by a disobliging word you silence the meanest, the gale will be less strong which is to bear up your esteem. And though nothing is so vain as the eager pursuit of empty applause, yet to be well thought of and to be kindly used by the world is like a glory about a woman's head' 'tis a perfumeshe carrieth about with her and leaveth wherever she goeth; 'tis a charm against ill-will. Malice may empty her quiver, but cannot wound; the dirt will not stick, the jests will not take."

Something of this charm is to be found in Peacock's heroines, so to call them.

George Meredith was Peacock's son-in-law, and learned more from Peacock than from any other writer; in his characters of women especially, and his convivial scenes.

There is, it has often been remarked a certain Gallic quality in Peacock's wit. It is gay and polished, and usually subtle. Our satirists are commonly heavy-weight prize-fighters. Our irony is often as strong as cheese. He has the spirit of wise mischief, like M. Anatole France.

---from *On Writing and Writers* by Walter Raleigh, being extracts from his note-books, selected and edited by George Gordon, London. (1926), pp. 151-54.

THE SATIRISTS
AND FANTASTICS

By Virginia Woolf
from
"Phases of Fiction" in *Granite and Rainbow*

THE CONFUSED feelings which the psychologists have roused in us, the extraordinary intricacy which they have revealed to us, the network of fine and scarcely intelligible yet profoundly interesting emotions in which they have involved us, set up a craving for relief, at first so primitive that it is almost a physical sensation. The mind feels like a sponge saturated full with sympathy and understanding; it needs to dry itself, to contract upon something hard. Satire and the sense that the satirist gives us that he has the world well within his grasp, so that it is at the mercy of his pen, precisely fulfil our needs.

A further instinct will lead us to pass over such famous satirists as Voltaire and Anatole France in favour of someone writing in our own tongue, writing English. For without any disrespect to the translator we have grown intolerably weary in reading Dostoevsky, as if we were reading with the wrong spectacles or as if a mist had formed between us and the page. We come to feel that every idea is slipping about in a suit badly cut and many sizes too large for it. For a translation makes us understand more clearly than the lectures of any professor the difference between raw words and written words; the nature and importance of what we call style. Even an inferior writer, using his own tongue upon his own ideas, works a change at once which is agreeable and remarkable. Under his pen the sentence shrinks and wraps itself firmly round the meaning, if it be but a little one. The loose, the baggy, shrivels up. And while a writer of passable English will do this, a writer like Peacock does infinitely more.

When we open *Crotchet Castle* and read that first very long sentence which begins, 'In one of those beautiful valleys, through which the Thames (not yet polluted by the tide, the scouring of cities or even the minor defilement of the sandy streams of Surrey)', it would be difficult to describe the relief it gives us, except metaphorically. First there is the shape which recalls something visually delightful, like a flowing wave or the lash of a whip vigorously flung; then as phrase joins phrase and one parenthesis after another pours in its tributary, we have a sense of the whole swimming stream gliding beneath old walls with the shadows of ancient buildings and the glow of green lawns reflected in it. And what is even more delightful after the immensities and obscurities in which we have been living, we are in a world so manageable in scale that we can take its measure, tease it and ridicule it. It is like stepping out into the garden on a perfect September morning when every shadow is sharp and every colour bright after a night of storm and thunder. Nature has submitted to the direction of man. Man himself is dominated by his intelligence. Instead of being manysided, complicated, elusive, people possess one idiosyncrasy apiece, which crystallizes them into sharp separate characters, colliding briskly when they meet. They seem ridiculously and grotesquely simplified out of all knowledge. Dr. Folliott, Mr. Firedamp, Mr. Skionar, Mr. Chainmail, and the rest seem after the tremendous thickness and bulk of the Guermantes and the Stavrogins nothing but agreeable caricatures which a clever old scholar has cut out of a sheet of black paper with a pair of scissors. But on looking closer we find that though it would be absurd to credit Peacock with any desire or perhaps capacity to explore the depths of the soul, his reticence is not empty but suggestive. The character of Dr. Folliott is drawn in three strokes of the pen. What lies between is left out. But each stroke indicates the mass behind it, so that the reader can make it out for himself; while it has, because of this apparent simplicity, all the sharpness of a caricature. The world so happily constituted that theTe is always trout for breakfast, wine in the cellar, and some amusing contretemps, such as the cook setting herself alight and being put out by the footman, to make us laugh---a world where there is nothing more pressing to do than to 'glide over the face of the waters, discussing everything and settling nothing', is not the world of pure fantasy; -it is close enough to be a parody of our world and to make our own follies and the solemnities of our institutions look a little silly.

The satirist does not, like the psychologist, labour under the oppression of omniscience. He has leisure to play with his mind freely, ironically. His sympathies are not deeply engaged. His sense of humour is not submerged.

But the prime distinction lies in the changed attitude towards reality. In the psychologists the huge burden of facts is based upon a firm foundation of dinner, luncheon, bed and breakfast. It is with surprise, yet with relief and a start of pleasure, that we accept Peacock's version of the world, which ignores so much, simplifies so much, gives the old globe a spin and shows another face of it on the other side. It is unnecessary to be quite so painstaking, it seems. And, after all, is not this quite as real, as true as the other? And perhaps all this posher about 'reality' is overdone. The great gain is perhaps that our relation with things is more distant. We reap the benefit of a more poetic point of view. A line like the charming 'At Godstow, they gathered hazel on the grave of Rosamond' could be written only by a writer who was at a certain distance from his people, so that there need be no explanations. For certainly with Trollope's people explanations would have been necessary; we should have wanted to know what they had been doing, gathering hazel, and where they had gone for dinner afterwards and how the carriage had met them. 'They', however, being Chainmail, Skionar, and the rest, are at liberty to gather hazel on the grave of Rosamond if they like; as they are free to sing a song if it so pleases them or to debate the march of mind.

The romantic took the same liberty but for another purpose. In the satirist we get not a sense of wildness and the soul's adventures, but that the mind is free and therefore sees through and dispenses with much that is taken seriously by writers of another calibre. There are, of course, limitations, reminders, even in the midst of our pleasure, of boundaries that we must not pass. We cannot imagine in the first place that the writer of such exquisite sentences can cover many reams of paper; they cost too much to make. Then again a writer who gives us so keen a sense of his own personality by the shape of his phrase is limited. We are always being brought into touch, not with Peacock himself, as with Trollope himself (for there is no giving away of his own secrets; he does not conjure up the very shape of himself and the sound of his laughter as Trollope does), but all the time our thought is taking the colour of his thought, we are insensibly thinking in his measure. If we write, we try to write in his manner, and this brings us into far greater intimacy,with him than with writers like Trollope again or Scott, who wrap their thought up quite adequately in a duffle grey blanket which wears well and suits everything. This may in the end, of course, lead to some restriction. Style may carry with it, especially in prose, so much personality that it keeps us within the range of that personality. Peacock pervades his book. . . .

---from "The Satirists and Fantastics," a section of the long essay, "Phases of Fiction" in *Granite and Rainbow* Essays by Virginia Woolf, London. (1958), pp. 130-33. The essay originally appeared in *The Bookman* April, May, & June, 1929.

THE LEGEND OF SAINT LAURA

(from *Gryll Grange* Ch. XXXIV.)

Saint Laura, in her sleep of death,
  Preserves beneath the tomb
---'Tis willed where what is willed must be---
In incorruptibility
  Her beauty and her bloom.

So pure her maiden life had been,
  So free from earthly stain,
'Twas fixed in fate by Heaven's own Queen,
That till the earth's last closing scene
  She should unchanged remain.

Within a deep sarcophagus
  Of alabaster sheen,
With sculptured lid of roses white,
She slumbered in unbroken night
  By mortal eyes unseen.

Above her marble couch was reared
  A monumental shrine,
Where cloistered sisters, gathering round,
Made night and morn the aisle resound
  With choristry divine.

The abbess died: and in her pride
    Her parting mandate said,
They should her final rest provide,
The alabaster couch beside,
    Where slept the sainted dead.

The abbess came of princely race:
    The nuns might not gainsay:
And sadly passed the timid band,
To execute the high command
    They dared not disobey.

The monument was opened then:
    It gave to general sight
The alabaster couch alone:
But all its lucid substance shone
    With præ.ternatural light.

They laid the corpse within the shrine:
    They closed its doors again:
But nameless terror seemed to fall,
Throughout the live-long night, on all
    Who formed the funeral train.

Lo! on the morrow morn, still closed
    The monument was found:
But in its robes funereal drest,
The corpse they had consigned to rest
    Lay on the stony ground.

So pure her maiden life had been,
    So free from earthly stain,
'Twas fixed in fate by Heaven's own Queen,
That till the earth's last closing scene
    She should unchanged remain.

Fear and amazement seized on all:
    They salled on Mary's aid:
And in the tomb, unclosed again,
With choral hymn and funeral train,
    The corpse again was laid.

So was it found when morning beamed:
    In solemn suppliant strain,
The nuns implored all saints in heaven,
That rest might to the corpse be given,
    Which they entombed again.

On the third night a watch was kept
    By many a friar and nun:
Trembling, all knelt in fervebt parayer,
Till on the dreary midnight air
    Rolled the deep bell-toll, "One!"

The saint within the opening tomb
    Like marble statue stood:
All fell to earth in deep dismay:
And through their ranks she passed away,
    In calm unchanging mood.

No answering sound her footsteps raised
    Along the stony floor:
Silent as death, severe as fate,
She glided through the chapel gate,
    And none beheld her more.

The alabaster couch was gone:
    The tomb was void and bare:
For the last time, with hasty rite,
Even 'mid the terror of the night,
    They laid the abbess there.

'Tis said, the abbess rests not well
    In that sepulchral pile:
But yearly, when the night comes round,
And dies of "One" the bell's deep sound
    She flits along the aisle.

But whither passed the virgin saint,
    To slumber far away,
Destined by Mary to endure,
Unfettered in her semblance pure,
    Until the judgement day?

None knew, and none may ever know:
    Angels the secret keep:
Impenetrable ramparts bound,
Eternal silence dwells around,
    The chamber of her sleep.

THE MONKS OF ST. MARK

'Tis midnight: the sky is with clouds overcast;
The forest-trees bend in the loud-rushing blast;
The rain strongly beats on these time-hallow'd spires;
The lightning pours swiftly its blue-pointed fires;
Triumphant the tempest-fiend rides in the dark,
And howls round the old abbey-walls of St. Mark!

The thunder, whose roaring the trav'ller appals,
Seems as if with the ground it would level the walls:
But in vain pours the *storm-king* this horrible rout;
The uproar within drowns the uproar without;
For the friars, with Bacchus, not Satan, to grapple,
The refect'ry have met in, instead of the chapel.

'Stead of singing *Te Deums*, on ground-pressing knees,
They were piously bawling songs, catches, and glees:
Or, all speakers, no hearers, unceasing, untir'd,
Each stoutly held forth, by the spirit inspir'd,
Till the Abbot, who only the flock could controul,
Exclaim'd: "Augustine! pr'ythee push round the bowl!"

The good brother obey'd; but, oh direful mishap!
Threw its scalding contents in Jeronimo's lap!
And o'er his bare feet as the boiling tide stream'd,
Poor Augustine fretted, Jeronimo scream'd,
While Pedro protested, it vex'd him infernally,
To see such good beverage taken "*externally!*"

The Abbot, Francisco, then feelingly said:
"Let that poor wounded devil be carried to bed:
And let Augustine, who, I boldly advance,
Is the whole and sole cause of this fatal mischance,
If e'er to forgiveness he dare to aspire,
Now bear to his cell the unfortunate friar."

He rose to obey, than a snail rather quicker,
But, finding his strength much diminish'd by liquor,
Declar'd, with a hiccup, he scarcely could stand,
And begged brother Pedro to *lend him a hand*.
Brother Pedro consented, but all was not right,
Till Nicholas offer'd to carry a light.

By the head and the feet then their victim they held,
Who with pain and with fear most tremendously yell'd;
And with one little lamp that scarce shone through the gloom,
In path curvilinear march'd out of the room,
And, unheeding the sound of the rain and the blast,
Through the long dismal corridor fearlessly pass'd.

From the right to the left, from the left to the right
Brother Nicholas reel'd, inconsiderate wight!
For not seeing the stairs to the hall-floor that led,
Instead of his heels he soon stood on his head:
He rolls to the bottom, the lamp-flame expires,
And darkness envelopes the wondering friars!

He squall'd, for the burning oil pour'd on his hand;
Bewilder'd did Pedro and Augustine stand:
Then loud roar'd the thunder, and Pedro in dread,
Abandon'd his hold of Jeronimo's head,
And Prone on the floor fell this son of the cowl,
And howl'd, deeply-smarting, a terrible howl!

Poor Augustine's bosom with terror was cold,
On finding his burthen thus slide from his hold:
Then, cautiously stealing, and groping around,
He felt himself suddenly struck to the ground;
Yells, groans, and strange noises, were heard in the dark,
And, trembling and sweating, he pray'd to St. Mark I

Meanwhile, the good Abbot was *boosing about*;
When, a little alarm'd by the tumult without,
Occasion'd by poor Brother Nich'las's fall
From the corridor-stairs to the floor of the hall,
Like a true jolly friend of good orderly laws,
He serpentin'd out to discover the cause.

Bewilder'd by liquor, by haste, and by fright,
He forgot that he stood in great need of a light;
When hiccuping, reeling, and curving along,
And humming a stave of a jolly old song,
He receiv'd a rude shock from an object unseen,
For he came in full contact with *Saint* Augustine!

By Jeronimo's carcase tripp'd up unawares,
He was instantly hurl'd down the corridor-stairs;
Brother Nicholas there, from the floor cold and damp,
Was rising with what yet remain'd of his lamp;
And, the worthy superior's good supper to spoil,
Regal'd his strange guest with a mouthful of oil!

Thence sprung the dire tumult, which, rising so near,
Had fill'd Augustine with confusion and fear:
But the sons of St. Mark, now appearing wit tapers,
At once put an end to his pray'rs and his vapors;
They reel'd back to their bowls, laugh'd at care and foul weather,
And were shortly all under the table together.

[*The Monks of St. Mark* was written (and perhaps published) in 1804]

A SELECTION OF
POEMS FROM MELINCOURT

THE TOMB OF LOVE

BY THE mossy weed-flowered column,
  Where the setting moonbeam's glance
Streams a radiance cold and solemn
  On the haunts of old romance:
Know'st thou what those shafts betoken,
  Scattered on that tablet lone,
Where the ivory bow lies broken
  By the monumental stone?

When true knighthood's shield, neglected,
  Mouldered in the empty hall;
When the charms that shield protected
  Slept in death's eternal thrall;
When chivalric glory perished
  Like the pageant of a dream,
Love in vain its memory cherished,
  Fired in vain the minstrel's theme.

Falsehood to an elvish minion
  Did the form of Love impart:

Cunning plumed its vampire pinion;
  Avarice tipped its golden dart.
Love, the hideous phantom flying,
  Hither came, no more to rove:
There his broken bow is Iying
  On that stone the tomb of Love!

GLEE---THE GHOSTS

IN LIFE three ghostly friars were we,
And now three friarly ghosts we be.
Around our shadowy table placed,
The spectral bowl before us floats:
With wine that none but ghosts can taste,
We wash our unsubstantial throats.
Three merry ghosts--three merry ghosts--
   three merry ghosts are we:
Let the ocean be Port, and we'll think it good sport
To be laid in that Red Sea.

With songs that jovial spectres chaunt,
Our old refectory still we haunt.
The traveller hears our midnight mirth:
"O list!" he cries, "the haunted choir!
"The merriest ghost that walks the earth, "
"Is sure the ghost of a ghostly friar."
Three merry ghosts--three merry ghosts--
   three merry ghosts are we:
Let the ocean be Port, and we'll think it good sport
To be laid in that Red Sea.

BALLAD TERZETTO

THE LADY, THE KNIGHT, AND THE FRIAR.

THE LADY.
O cavalier! what dost thou here,
Thy tuneful vigils keeping;
While the northern star looks cold from far
And half the world is sleeping?

THE KNIGHT.
O lady! here, for seven long year,
Have I been nightly sighing,
Without the hope of a single tear
To pity me were I dying.

THE LADY.
Should I take thee to have and to hold,
Who hast nor lands nor money?
Alas! 'tis only in flowers of gold
That married bees flnd honey.

THE KNIGHT.
O lady fair! to my constant prayer
Fate proves at last propitious;
And bags of gold in my hand I bear,
And parchment scrolls delicious.

THE LADY.
My maid the door shall open throw,

For we too long have tarried:
The friar keeps watch in the cellar below,
And we will at once be married.

   THE FRIAR.

My children! great is Fortune's power;
And plain this truth appears,
That gold thrives more in a single hour,
Than love in seven long years.

THE FLOWER OF LOVE

'TIS SAID the rose is Love's own flower,
Its blush so bright, its thorns so many;
And winter on its bloom has power,
But has not on its sweetness any.
For though young Love's ethereal rose
Will droop on Age's wintry bosom,
Yet still its faded leaves disclose
The fragrance of their earliest blossom.

But ah! the fragrance lingering there
Is like the sweets that mournful duty
Bestows with sadly-soothing care,
To deck the grave of bloom and beauty.
For when its leaves are shrunk and dry,
Its blush extinct, to kindle never,
That fragrance is but Memory's sigh,
That breathes of pleasures past for ever.

Why did not Love the amaranth choose,
That bears no thorns, and cannot perish ?
Alas! no sweets its flowers diffuse,
And only sweets Love's life can cherish.
But be the rose and amaranth twined,
And Love, their mingled powers assuming,
Shall round his brows a chaplet bind,
For ever sweet, for ever blooming.

TERZETTO

1.

HARK! o'er the silent waters stealing,
The dash of oars sounds soft and clear:
Through night's deep veil, all forms concealing,
Nearer it comes, and yet more near.

See! where the long reflection glistens,
In yon lone tower her watch-light burns:
To hear our distant oars she listens,
And, listtening, strikes the harp by turns.

The stars are bright, the skies unclouded;
No moonbeam shines; no breezes wake:
Is it my love, in darkness shrouded,
Whose dashing oar disturbs the lake?

2.

0 haste, sweet maid, the cords unrolling;
The holy hermit chides our stay!

1. 2. 3.

Hark! from his lonely islet tolling,
His midnight bell shall guide our way.

THE MORNING OF LOVE

O! THE spring-time of life is the season of blooming,
And the morning of love is the season of joy;
Ere noontide and summer, with radiance consuming,
Look down on their beauty, to parch and destroy.
0! faint are the blossoms life's pathway adorning,
When the first magic glory of hope is withdrawn;
For the flowers of the spring, and the light of the morning,
Have no summer budding, and no second dawn.

Through meadows all sunshine, and verdure, and flowers
The stream of the valley in purity flies;
But mixed with the tides, where some proud city lowers,
O! where is the sweetness that dwelt on its rise ?
The rose withers fast-on the breast it first graces;
Its beauty is fled ere the day be half done:--
And life is that stream which its progress defaces,
And love is that flower which can bloom but for one.

THE SUNDIAL

THE IVY o'er the mouldering wall
Spreads like a tree, the growth of years:
The wild wind through the doorless hall
A melancholy music rears,
A solitary voice, that sighs
O'er man's forgotten pageantries.
  Above the central gate, the clock,
Through clustering ivy dimly seen,
Seems, like the ghost of Time, to mock
The wrecks of power that once has been.
The hands are rusted on its face;
Even where they ceased, in years gone by,
To keep the flying moments pace;
Fixing, in Fancy's thoughtful eye,
A point of ages passed away,
A speck of time, that owns no tie
With aught that lives and breathes to-day.
  But 'mid the rank and towering grass,
Where breezes wave, in mournful sport,
The weeds that choke the ruined court,
The careless hours that circling pass,
Still trace upon the dialled brass
The shade of their unvarying way:
And evermore, with every ray
That breaks the clouds and gilds the air,
Time's stealthy steps are imaged there:
Even as the long-revolving years
In self-reflecting circles flow,
From the first bud the hedge-row bears,

To wintry Nature's robe of snow.
The changeful forms of mortal things
Decay and pass; and art and power
Oppose in vain the doom that flings
Oblivion on their closing hour:
While still, to every woodland vale,
New blooms, new fruits, the seasons bring,
For other eyes and lips to hail
With looks and sounds of welcoming:
As where some stream light-eddying roves
By sunny meads and shadowy groves,
Wave following wave departs for ever,
But still flows on the eternal river.

QUINTETTO

MR. FEATHERNEST, MR. VAMP, MR. KILLTHEDEAD, MR.
PAPERSTAMP, AND MR. ANYSIDE ANTIJACK.

To the tune of
"Turning, turning, turning, as wheel goes round."

RECITATIVE. MR. PAPERSTAMP.
Jack Horner's CHRISTMAS PIE my learned nurse
Interpreted to mean the *public purse.*
From thence a *plum* he drew. O happy Horner!
Who would not be ensconced in thy snug corner

THE FIVE.
While round the public board all eagerly we linger,
for what we can get we will try, try, try:
And we'll all have a finger, a finger, a finger,
We'll all have a finger in the CHRISTMAS PIE.

MR. FEATHERNEST.
By my own poetic laws, I'm a dealer in applause
For those who don't deserve it, but will buy, buy
So round the court I linger, and thus I get a finget
A finger, finger, finger in the CHRISTMAS PIE.

THE FIVE.
And we'll all have a finger, a finger, a finger,
We'll all have a finger in the CHRISTMAS PIE.

31

MR. VAMP.
My share of pie to win, I will dash through thick and thin
And philosophy and liberty shall fly, fly, fly:
And truth and taste shall know, that their eve Iasting foe
Has a finger, finger, finger in the CHRISTMAS PIE.

THE FIVE.
And we'll all have a finger, a finger, a finger,
We'll all have a finger in the CHRISTMAS PIE.

MR. KILLTHEDEAD.
I'll make my verses rattle with the din of war and battle,
For war doth increase sa-la-ry, ry, ry:
And I'll shake the public ears with the triumph of Algiers,
And thus I ll get a finger in the CHRISTMAS PIE.

THE FIVE.
And we'll all have a finger, a finger, a finger,
We'll all have a finger in the CHRISTMAS PIE.

MR. PAPERSTAMP.
And while you thrive by ranting, I'll try my luck at canting,
And scribble verse and prose all so dry, dry, dry:
And Mystic's patent smoke public intellect shall choke,
Arld we ll all have a finger in the CHRISTMAS PIE.

THE FIVE.
We'll all have a finger, a finger, a finger,
We'll all have a finger in the CHRISTMAS PIE.

MR. ANYSIDE ANTIJACK.
My tailor is so clever, that my coat will turn for ever,
And take any colour you can dye, dye, dye:
For all my earthly wishes are among the loaves and fishes,
And to have my little finger in the CHRISTMAS PIE.

THE FIVE.
And we'll all have a finger, a finger, a finger,
We'll all have a finger in the CHRISTMAS PIE.

THE MAGIC BARK

I

O FREEDOM! power of life and light!
Sole nurse of truth and glory!
Bright dweller on the rocky cliff!
Lone wanderer on the sea!
Where'er the sunbeam slumbers bright
On snow-clad mountains hoary;
Wherever flies the veering skiff,
O'er waves that breathe of thee!
Be thou the guide of all my thoughtÑ
The source of all my beingÑ
The genius of my waking mind---
The spirit of my dreams!
To me thy magic spell be taught,
The captive spirit freeing,
To wander with the ocean-wind
Where'er thy beacon beams.

II

O! sweet it were, in magic bark,
On one loved breast reclining,
To sail around the varied world,
To every blooming shore;
And oft the gathering storm to mark
Its lurid folds combining;
And safely ride, with sails unfurled,
Amid the tempest's roar;
And see the mighty breakers rave
On cliff, and sand, and shingle,

And hear, with long re-echoing shock,
The caverned steeps reply;
And while the storm-cloud and the wave
In darkness seemed to mingle,
To skim beside the surf-swept rock,
And glide uninjured by.

III
And when the summer seas were calm,
And summer skies were smiling,
And evening came, with clouds of gold,
To gild the western wave;
And gentle airs and dews of balm,
The pensive mind beguiling,
Should call the Ocean Swain to fold
His sea-flocks in the cave,
Unearthly music's tenderest spell,
With gentlest breezes blending
And waters softly rippling near
The prow's light course along,
Should flow from Triton's winding shell,
Through ocean's depths ascending
From where it charmed the Nereid's ear,
Her coral bowers among.

IV
How sweet, where eastern Nature smiles,
With swift and mazy motion
Before the odour-breathing breeze
Of dewy morn to glide;
Or, 'mid the thousand emerald isles
That gem the southern ocean,
Where fruits and flowers, from loveliest trees,
O'erhang the slumbering tide:
Or up some western stream to sail,

To where its myriad fountains
Roll down their everlasting rills
From many a cloud-capped height,
Till mingling in some nameless vale,
'Mid forest-cinctured mountains,
The river-cataract shakes the hills
With vast and volumed might.

V

The poison-trees their leaves should shed,
The yellow snake should perish,
The beasts of blood should crouch and cower,
Where'er that vessel past:
All plagues of fens and vapours bred,
That tropic fervors cherish,
Should fly before its healing power,
Like mists before the blast.
Where'er its keel the strand imprest,
The young fruit's ripening cluster,
The bird's free song, its touch should greet,
The opening flower's perfume;
The streams zalong the green earth's breast
Should roll in purer lustre,
And love should heighten every sweet,
And brighten every bloom.

VI

And, Freedom! thy meridian blaze
Should chase the clouds that lower,
Wherever mental twilight dim
Obscures Truth's vestal flame,
Wherever Fraud and Slavery raise
The throne of blood-stained Power,
Wherever Fear and Ignorance hymn
Some fabled daemon's name!

The bard, where torrents thunder down
Beside thy burning altar,
Should kindle, as in days of old,
The mind's ethereal fire;
Ere yet beneath a tyrant's frown
The Muse's voice could falter,
Or Flattery strung with chords of gold
The minstrel's venal Iyre.

Melicourt was first published in 1817.

THE ROUND TABLE

OR
KING ARTHUR'S FEAST

INTRODUCTION

KING ARTHUR is said to have disappeared after the battle of Camlan, and to have never been seen again; which gave rise to a tradition, that he had been carried away by Merlin, a famous prophet and magician of his time, and would return to his kingdom at some future period.---The Welch continued to expect him for many hundred years; and it is by no means certain that they have entirely given him up. He is here represented as inhabiting a solitary island, under the influence of the prophet Merlin; by whose magic power he is shown all the kings and queens who have sat on his throne since his death, and giving to them a grand feast, at his old established round table, attended by their principal secretaries, dukes, lords, admirals, generals, poets, and a long train of courtiers. The kings are of course mentioned in the order of their succession. The allegory is illustrated as concisely as possible in the notes. So many histories of England being published for the use of young persons, we have only attached the names of the kings, and to such instances as might not be considered sufficiently explanatory.

KING ARTHUR'S FEAST

THE ROUND TABLE

KING ARTHUR sat down by the lonely sea-coast,
As thin as a lath, and as pale as a ghost:
He looked on the east, and the west, and the south,
With a tear in his eye, and a pipe in his mouth;
And he said to old Merlin, who near him did stand,
Drawing circles, triangles, and squares on the sand,
"Sure nothing more dismal and tedious can be,
Than to sit always smoking and watching the sea:
Say when shall the fates re-establish my reign,
And help my round-table in Britain again?"

  Old Merlin replied: "By my art it appears,
Not in less than three hundred and seventy years;
But in the mean time I am very well able
To spread in this island your ancient round table;
And to grace it with guests of unparallelled splendour,
I'll summon old Pluto forthwith to surrender
All the kings who have sat on your throne, from the day
When from Camlan's destruction I snatched you away."

  King Arthur's long face, by these accents restored,
Grew as round as his table, as bright as his sword;
While the wand of old Merlin waved over the ocean,
Soon covered its billows with brilliant commotion;
For ships of all ages and sizes appearing,
Towards the same shore were all rapidly steering,
Came cleaving the billows with sail and with oar,
Yacht, pinnace, sloop, frigate, and seventy-four.

King Arthur scarce spied them afar from the land,
Ere their keels were fixed deep in the yellow sea-sand;
And from under their canopies, golden and gay,
Came kings, queens, and courtiers, in gallant array,
Much musing and marvelling who it might be,
That was smoking his pipe by the side of the sea;
But Merlin stepped forth with a greeting right warm,
And then introduced them in order and form.

The Saxons [1] came first, the pre-eminence claiming,
With scarce one among them but Alfred worth naming.
Full slightly they looked upon Canute [2] the bold,
And remembered the drubbing he gave them of old:
Sad Harold [3] came last; and the crown which he wore
Had been broken, and trampled in dust and in gore.
Now the sun in the west had gone down to repose,
When before them at once a pavilion arose;
Where Arthur's round table was royally spread,
And illumined with lamps, purple, yellow, and red.
The smell of roast beef put them all in a foment,
So they scrambled for seats, and were ranged in a moment.

The Conqueror [4] stood up, as they thought, to say grace;
But he scowled round the board with a resolute face;
And the company stared, when he swore by the fates,
That a list he would have of their names and estates; [5]
And lest too much liquor their brains should inspire
To set the pavilion and table on fire,
He hoped they'd acknowledge he counselled right well,
To put out the lights when he tinkled his bell. [6]

His speech was cut short by a general dismay;
For William the Second [7] had fainted away,
At the smell of some New Forest venison [8] before him;
But a tweak on the nose, Arthur said, would restore him.

But another disturbance compelled him to mark
The pitiful state of Henry Beauclerk; [9]
Who had fallen on the lampreys with ardour so stout, [10]
That he dropped from his chair in the midst of the rout.
Arthur surprised at a king so voracious,
Thought a salt-water ducking might prove efficacious.

Now Stephen, [11] for whom some bold barons had carved,
[12]
Said, while some could get surfeited, he was half-starved:
For his arms were so pinioned, unfortunate elf! [13]
He could hit on no method of helping himself.

But a tumult more furious called Arthur to check it,
'Twixt Henry the Second [14] and Thomas a Becket. [15]
"Turn out," exclaimed Arthur, "that prelate so free,
And from the first rock see him thrown in the sea."
So they hustled out Becket without judge or jury,
Who quickly returned in a terrible fury.
The lords were enraged, and the ladies affrighted;
But his head was soon cracked in the fray he excited;
When in rushed some monks in a great perturbation,
And gave good King Henry a sound flagellation;
Which so cooly he took, that the president swore,
He ne'er saw such a bigoted milk-sop before.

But Arthur's good humour was quickly restored,
When to lion-hearted Richard [16] a bumper he poured
Whose pilgrim's array told the tale of his toils,
Half-veiling his arms and his Saracen spoils; [17]
As he sliced up the venison of merry Sherwood,
He told a long story of bold Robin Hood, [18]
Which gave good King Arthur such a hearty delight,
That he vow'd he'd make Robin a round-table knight.

41

While Merlin to fetch Robin Hood was preparing,
John Lackland [19] was blustering, and vapouring, and
swearing,
And seemed quite determined the roast to be ruling; [20]
But some stout fellows near him prepared him a cooling;
Who seized him, and held him, nor gave him release,
Till he signed them a bond for preserving the peace. [21]

While Henry the Third, [22] dull, contemned, and
forsaken,
Sat stupidly silent, regaling on Bacon, [23]
The First of the Edwards [24] charmed Arthur with tales
Of fighting in Palestine, Scotland, and Wales; [25]
But Merlin asserted his angry regards,
Recollecting how Edward had treated the Bards. [26]
The Second, [27] whose days in affliction had run, [28]
Sat pensive and sad 'twixt his father and son.
But on the Third Edward [29] resplendently glance
The blazons of knighthood, and trophies of France; [30]
Beside him his son in black armour appears,
That yet bears the marks of the field of Poictiers. [31]

From the festival's pomp, and the table's array,
Pale Richard of Bordeaux [32] turned sadly away;
The thought of that time his remembrance appals,
When Famine scowled on him in Pomfret's dark walls. [33]

Beside him sat Bolinbroke, [34] gloomy and stern,
Nor dared his dark eyes on his victim to turn; [35]
The wrinkles of care o'er his features were spread,
And thorns lined the crown that encircled his head. [36]

But Harry of Monmouth [37] some guests had brought in,
Who drank so much liquor, and made such a din, [38]
(While Arthur full loudly his mirth did disclose

42

At Falstaff's fat belly and Bardolph's red nose)
That he turned them all out with monarchial pride, [39]
And laid the plumed cap of his revels aside,
And put on the helmet, and breastplate, and shield,
That did such great service on Agincourt's field. [40]

And now rang the tent with unusual alarms,
For the white and red roses were calling to arms; [41]
Confusion and tumult established their reign,
And Arthur stood up, and called silence in vain.

Poor Harry the Sixth, [42] hustled, beaten, and prest,
Had his nosegay of lilies [43] soon torn from his breast;
And, though Margaret, to shield him, had clasped him
around, [44]
From her arms he was shaken, and hurled to the ground; [45]
While Edward of York [46] flourished over his head
The rose's pale blossoms, and trampled the red;
Though Warwick strove vainly the ill to repair,
And set fallen Henry again on his chair.

The children [47] of Edward stood up in the fray,
But, touched by cruel Richard, [48] they vanished away;
Who, knowing none loved him, resolved all should fear
him,
And therefore knocked every one down who was near him.
Till him in his turn Harry Richmond [49] assailed,
And at once, on his downfall, good order prevailed;
And Richmond uplifted, to prove the strife ended,
A wreath where the white and red roses were blended. [50]

With his Jane, and his Annes, and his Catherines beside,
Sat Henry the Eighth, [51] in true Ottoman pride,
And quaffed of with Wolsey the goblet's red tide;

But over the head of each lady so fair
An axe was impending, that hung by a hair. [52]

Bold Arthur, whose fancy this king had not won,
Look'd with hope and delight on young Edward [53] his son;
But had scarcely commended his learning and grace,
Ere he found his attention called off [54] to the place
Where the infamous Marg [55] polluted the feast,
Who sat drinking blood from the skull of a priest. [56]

But he struggled his horror and rage to repress,
And sought consolation from worthy Queen Bess, [57]
Who had brought Drake and Raleigh her state to sustain, [58]
With American spoils and the trophies of Spain;
While Shakspeare and Spenser, [59] with song and with fable,
Enchanted King Arthur and all round his table.

Now the First of the James's [60] complained of the heat,
And seemed ill at ease on his ricketty seat;
It proved, when examined (which made them all stare),
A gunpowder barrel instead of a chair. [61]

The First of the Charles's [62] was clearing the dishes,
Taking more than his share of the loaves and the fishes, [63]
Not minding at all what the company said,
When up started Cromwell, and sliced off his head. [64]

Charles the Second, [65] enraged at the villainous deed,
Tried to turn out old Cromwell, but could not succeed;
But he mastered young Dick, and then cooled his own wrath
In syllabub, trifle, and fillagree broth. [66]

James the Second, [67] with looks full of anger and gloom,
Pronounced nothing good but the cookery of Rome; [68]

So begged of King Arthur, his dear royal crony,
To make all the company eat Macaroni; [69]
But Arthur bade Mary an orange present, [70]
At which James grew queasy, and fled from the tent.
So she placed on his seat honest William, [71] her spouse,
And with laurel and olive encircled his brows; [72]
Wreath of glory and peace, by young Freedom entwined,
And gave him a key to the lock [73] of the mind.

Now as Arthur continued the party to scan,
He did not well know what to make of Queen Anne; [74]
But Marlborough, [75] he saw, did her credit uplift,
And he heartily laughed at the jokes of Dean Swift. [76]

Then shook hands with two Georges, [77] who near him
were seated,
Who closed in his left, and the circle completed;
He liked them both well, but he frankly averred,
He expected to prove better pleased with the Third.

NOTES

[*The Round Table* was first published in 1817, by John Arliss
(London), without authorial attribution;. the *Edinburgh
Review* for November 1817, however, lists it with other new
publications as written 'by the author of "Sir Hornbook."'
Notes in brackets have been added by Informal]

1 The Saxons invaded England, and dispossessed the
Britons. The most famous of the saxon Kings was Alfred.
[The kings who succeeded Alfred the Great (reigned from
871 to 899) were: Edward the Elder (899-924); Athelstan
(924-39); Edmund (939-46); Edred (946-55); Edwy (955-59);
Edgar the Peaceful (959-75); Edward the Martyr (975-78);
Ethelred II (978-1016); Cnut (1016-35); Harold I (1035-40);
Harthacnut (1040-42); Edward the Confessor (1042-1066);
and Harold II (1066).]

2 The Danes, under Canute, conquered the Saxons. The
sons of Canute died without children, and the government
returned to the Saxon kings.

3 The last of the Saxon kings was Harold II, who was killed
in the battle of Hastings, when William, Duke of Normandy,
gained a decisive victory [on 14 October 1066].

4 William I, the Conqueror [reigned 1066-87].

5 Doomsday Book.

6 The curfew. [Curfew comes from the Old French, *couvre-
feu*--literally, cover fire.]

7 William II. Rufus [1087-1100].

8 Accidentally killed by an arrow while hunting in the New Forest.

9 Henry I. Beauclerk [1100-35].

10 Died eating lampreys.

11 Stephen, of Bloix [1135-54].

12 Held in subjection by the barons.

13 And so restricted his authority, that he had little more than the name of a king.

14 Henry II. Fitz-Empress [1154-89].

15 Quarrelled with his minister, Thomas a Becket, Archbishop of Canterbury, who was compelled to fly the country; but afterwards returning, was murdered [on 29 December, 1170] by some followers of the king; for which Henry was forced to do penance, and was whipped by the monks at Becket's tomb.

16 Richard Coeur-de-Lion [1189-99].

17 Returned in a pilgrim's disguise through Europe from his wars in the Holy Land.

18 In his time lived Robin Hood, the celebrated robber of Sherwood Forest.

19 King John, surnamed Lackland [1199-1216].

20 Ambitious of absolute power.

21 Forced by his barons to sign Magna Carta.

22 Henry III. of Winchester [1216-72].

23 A weak and foolish king, in whose reign lived Friar [Roger] Bacon.

24 Edward I. Longshanks [1272-1307].

25 Gained many victories.

26 Massacred the Welch Bards.

27 Edward II. of Caernarvon [1307-27].

28 Murdered by his wife's knowledge in Berkley Castle.

29 Edward III [1327-77].

30 Conquered France in conjunction with his son, the Black Prince.

31 The Battle of Poictiers [19 Sept., 1356].

32 Richard II. of Bordeaux [1377-99].

33 Killed in Pomfret Castle.

34 Henry IV. Bolinbroke [1399-1413].

35 Obtained the crown by rebelling against Richard II.

36 Was miserable all his reign.

37 Henry V. of Monmouth [1413-22].

38 Led a very dissolute life while Prince of Wales, and kept a set of drunken companions, to whom Shakspeare has given the names of Falstaff, Bardolph, &c.

39 Discarded them when he came to be king.

40 And gained great victories in France, particularly the battle of Agincourt

41 The civil wars of York and Lancaster, of which respective pArties the white and red roses were the emblems.

42 Henry VI. of Windsor [1422-61 & 1470-71].

43 Lost the kingdom of France.

44 Supported by his queen, Margaret [of Anjou].

45 Overcome by the York party, and made a prisoner in the Tower.

46 Edward IV., raised to the throne by the aid of the Earl of Warwick; who afterwards quarrelled with Edward, and endeavoured to restore Henry, but without success.

47 Edward V. [1483] and his brother, the Duke of York, died while children, supposed to have been murdered in the Tower by order of their uncle Richard.

48 Richard III., a cruel and sanguinary tyrant [1483-85].

49 Conquered in the battle of Bosworth by Henry of Richmond, afterwards Henry VII. [1485-1509]

50 Being himself of the house of Lancaster, married

Elizabeth, sister of Edward V., who was of the house of York; thus uniting the two houses, and ending the civil wars.

51 Henry VIII. {1509-47]

52 Had six wives--one Jane, two Annes, and three Catherines, in the following order:

    1 Catherine of Aragon, whom he divorced.
    2 Anne Boleyn, whom he beheaded.
    3 Jane Seymour, who died in giving birth to Edward VI.
    4 Anne of Cleves, whom he sent back to her parents.
    5 Catherine Howard, whom he beheaded.
    6 Catherine Parr, who outlived him.

53 Edward VI. a very promising young prince [1547-58].

54 Died in his sixteenth year.

55 Mary [I (1553-58)]. Cruel Queen Mary. Daughter of Henry the Eighth.

56 Burned three hundred persons for not being of her opinion in religion.

57 Elizabeth [I (1558-1603)] A wise and fortunate queen.

58 Her Admirals, among whom were Sir Francis Drake and Sir Walter Raleigh, sailed round the world, settled colonies in North America, defeated the Spanish Armada, &c.

59 In her reign lived many eminent authors, particularly Shakspeare and Spenser.

60 James the First [of England (1603-25) and Sixth of the

Scots from 1567].

61 The gunpowder plot, 5th November, 1605.

62 Charles I. [1625-49]

63 Overstrained his prerogative; encroached on the liberties of the people, and on the privileges of parliament. The consequence was a civil war and the loss of his head.

64 The commonwealth succeeded, at the head of which was Oliver Cromwell. He was succeeded by his son Richard, who was displaced by the restoration of Charles II.

65 Charles II. [1660-85]

66 A frivolous and dissolute king.

67 James II. [and VII (1685-88)]

68 A bigoted Roman Catholic.

69 Used violent measures to establish that religion in England.

70 Was obliged to fly the country; and the crown devolved to his daughter Mary [II. (1689-94)], and her husband, William, Prince of Orange.

71 William III. [and II of Scotland (1689-1702)]

72 His reign was distinguished by foreign victories and domestic prosperity.

73 By being the origin of the present form of the English

constitution, in the glorious revolution of 1688; and by the life and writings of the philosopher Locke.

74 Anne [1702-14].

75 Her general, the Duke of Marlborough, gained several victories in France.

76 Many eminent literary characters flourished in her time, particularly Swift and Pope.

77 The House of Hanover.
    George I. [1714-27]
    George II. [1727-60]
    George III. [1760-1820]

PALMYRA

(1ST EDITION)

---anankta ton pantôn huperbal-
lonta chronon makarôn.

Pind[ar. *Hymn.* frag. 33].

PALMYRA

I

As the mountain-torrent rages,
Loud, impetuous, swift, and strong,
So the rapid streams of ages
Rolls with ceaseless tide along.
Man's little day what clouds o'ercast!
How soon his longest day is past!
All-conquering DEATH, in solemn date unfurl'd,
    Comes, like the burning desert blast,
    And sweeps him from the world.
The noblest works of human pow'r
In vain resist the fate-fraught hour;
The marble hall, the rock-built tow'r,
    Alike submit to destiny:
OBLIVION's awful storms resound;

53

The massy columns fall around;
The fabric totters to the ground,
    And darkness veils its memory!

II

'Mid SYRIA's barren world of sand,
    Where THEDMOR's marble wastes expand.
Where DESOLATION, on the blasted plain,
    Has fix'd his adamantine throne,
    I mark, in silence and alone,
        His melancholy reign.
These silent wrecks, more eloquent than speech,
    Full many a tale of awful note impart;
Truths more sublime than bard or sage can teach
    This pomp of ruin presses on the heart.
        Whence rose that dim, mysterious sound,
        That breath'd in hollow murmurs round?
            As sweeps the gale
            Along the vale,
        Where many a mould'ring tomb is spread,
            Awe-struck, I hear,
            In fancy's ear,
        The voices of th' illustrious dead:
As slow they pass along, they seem to sigh,
"Man, and the works of man, are only born to die!"

III

As scatter'd round, a dreary space,
    Ye spirits of the wise and just!
In reverential thought I trace
    The mansions of your sacred dust,
    Enthusiast FANCY, rob'd in light,
Pours on the air her many-sparkling rays,
Redeeming from OBLIVION's deep'ning night

54

The deeds of ancient days.
The mighty forms of chiefs of old,
To VIRTUE dear, and PATRIOT TRUTH sublime,
    In feeble splendor I behold,
Discover'd dimly through the mists of TIME,
As through the vapours of the mountain-stream
With pale reflection glows the sun's declining beam.

                IV
Still as twilight's mantle hoary
    Spreads progressive on the sky,
See, in visionary glory,
    Darkly-thron'd, they sit on high.
But whose the forms, oh FAME, declare,
That crowd majestic on the air?
Bright Goddess! come, on rapid wings,
To tell the mighty deeds of kings.
        Where art thou, FAME?
        Each honor'd name
From thy eternal roll unfold:
        Awake the lyre,
        In songs of fire,
To chiefs renown'd in days of old.
        I call in vain!
        The welcome strain
Of praise to them no more shall sound:
        Their actions bright
        Must sleep in night,
Till TIME shall cease his mystic round.
The dazzling glories of their day
The stream of years has swept away;
Their names, that struck the foe with fear,
Shall ring no more on mortal ear!

                55

V

Yet faithful MEMORY's raptur'd eye
Can still the godlike form descry,
  Of him, who, on EUPHRATES' shore,
From SAPOR's brow his blood-stain'd laurels tore,
And bade the ROMAN banner stream unfurl'd;
  When the stern GENIUS of the startling waves
    Beheld on PERSIA s host of slaves
      Tumultuous ruin hurl'd!
Meek SCIENCE too, and TASTE refin'd,
  The grave with deathless flow'rs have dress'd,
Of him whose virtue-kindling mind
  Their ev'ry charm supremely bless'd;
Who trac'd the mazy warblings of the lyre
With all a critic's art, and all a poet's fire.

VI

Where is the bard, in these degen'rate days,
  To whom the muse the blissful meed awards,
Again the dithyrambic song to raise,
  And strike the golden harp's responsive chords?
  Be his alone the song to swell,
  The all-transcendent praise to tell
    Of yon immortal form,
  That bursting through the veil of years,
  In changeless majesty appears,
Bright as the sun-beams thro' the scatt'ring storm!
    What countless charms around her rise!
    What dazzling splendor sparkles in her eyes!
      On her radiant brow enshrin'd,
MINERVA's beauty blends with JUNO's grace;
  The matchless virtues of her godlike mind
Are stamp'd conspicuous on her angel-face.

VII

Hail, sacred shade, to NaATURE dear!
Though sorrow clos'd thy bright career,
Though clouds obscur'd thy setting day,
Thy fame shall never pass away!
Long shall the mind's unfading gaze
Retrace thy pow'r's meridian blaze,
When o'er ARABIAN deserts, vast and wild,
And EGYPT s land, (where REASON's wakeful eye
First on the birth of ART and SCIENCE smil'd,
And bade the shades of mental darkness fly)
And o'er ASSYRIA's many-peopled plains,
By Justice led, thy conqu'ring armies pour'd,
When humbled nations kiss'd thy silken chains,
Or fled dismay'd from zABDAS ' victor-sword:
Yet vain the hope to share the purple robe,
Or snatch from ROMAN arms the empire of the globe.

VIII

Along the wild and wasted plain
His veteran bands the ROMAN monarch led,
And rolled his burning wheels o'er heaps of slain:
The prowling chacal heard afar
The devastating yell of war,
And rush'd, with gloomy howl, to banquet on the dead!

IX

For succour to PALMYRA's walls
Her trembling subjects fled, confounded,
But wide amid her regal halls
The whirling fires resounded.
Onward the hostile legions pour'd:
Nor beauteous youth, nor helpless age,
Nor female charms, by savage breasts ador'd,
Could check the ROMAN's barb'rous rage,

Or blunt the murd'rous sword.
Loud, long, and fierce, the voice of slaughter roar'd,
The night-shades fell, the work of death was o'er,
PALMYRA's sun had set, to rise no more!

X

What mystic form, uncouth and dread,
With wither'd cheek, and hoary head,
Swift as the death-fire cleaves the sky,
Swept on sounding pinions by?
'Twas TIME: I know the FOE OF KINGS,
His scythe, and sand, and eagle wings:
He cast a burning look around,
And wav'd his bony hand, and frown'd.
Far from the spectre's scowl of fire
FANCY's feeble forms retire,
Her air-born phantoms melt away,
Like stars before the rising day.

XI

Yes, all are flown!
I stand alone,
At ev'ning's calm and pensive hour,
Mid wasted domes,
And mould'ring tombs,
The wrecks of vanity and pow'r.
One shadowy tint enwraps the plain;
No form is near, no sounds intrude,
To break the melancholy reign
Of silence and of solitude.
How oft, in scenes like these, since TIME began,
With downcast eye has CONTEMPLATION trod,
Far from the haunts of FOLLY, VICE, and MAN,
To hold sublime communion with her GOD!
How oft, in scenes like these, the pensive sage

Has mourn'd the hand of FATE, severely just,
WAR's wasteful course, and DEATH's unsparing rage,
And dark OBLIVION, frowning in the dust!
Has mark'd the tombs, that king's o'erthrown declare,
Just wept their fall, and sunk to join them there!

XII

In yon proud fane, majestic in decay,
  How oft of old the swelling hymn arose,
In loud thanksgiving to the LORD OF DAY,
  Or pray'r for vengeance on triumphant foes!
    'Twas there, ere yet AURELIAN's hand
    Had kindled Ruin's smould'ring brand,
    As slowly mov'd the sacred choir
    Around the altar's rising fire,
    The priest, with wild and glowing eye,
    Bade the flow'r-bound victim die;
    And while he fed the incense-flame,
      With many a holy mystery,
    Prophetic inspiration came
      To teach th' impending destiny,
    And shook his venerable frame
      With most portentous augury!
    In notes of anguish, deep and slow,
    He told the coming hour of woe;
    The youths and maids, with terror pale,
    In breathless torture heard the tale,
      And silence hung
      On ev'ry tongue,
    While thus the voice prophetic rung:

XIII

"Whence was the hollow scream of fear,
Whose tones appall'd my shrinking ear?
Whence was the modulated cry,

That seem'd to swell, and hasten by?
What sudden blaze illum'd the night?
Ha! 'twas DESTRUCTION's meteor-light!
Whence was the whirlwind's eddying breath?
Ha! 'twas the fiery blast of DEATH!

XIV

See! the mighty God of Battle
  Spreads abroad his crimson train!
Discord's myriad voices rattle
  O'er the terror-shaken plain.
Banners stream, and helmets glare,
Show'ring arrows hiss in air;
Echoing through the darken'd skies,
Wildly-mingling murmurs rise,
The clash of splendor-beaming steel,
  The buckler ringing hollowly,
The cymbal's silver-sounding peal,
  The last deep groan of agony,
    The hurrying feet
    Of wild retreat,
The lengthening shout of victory!

XV

"O'er our plains the vengeful stranger
  Pours, with hostile hopes elate:
Who shall check the coming danger?
  Who escape the coming fate?
Thou! that through the heav'ns afar,
  When the shades of night retire,
Proudly roll'st thy shining car,
  Clad in sempiternal fire!
Thou! from whose benignant light
  Fiends of darkness, strange and fell,
Urge their ebon-pinion'd flight

To the central caves of hell!
Sun ador'd! attend our call!
Must thy favor'd people fall?
Must we leave our smiling plains,
To groan beneath the stranger's chains ?
Rise, supreme in heav'nly pow'r,
On our foes destruction show'r;
Bid thy fatal arrows fly,
Till their armies sink and die;
Through their adverse legions spread
Pale Disease, and with'ring Dread,
Wild Confusion's fev'rish glare,
Horror, Madness, and Despair!

XVI
"Woe to thy numbers fierce and rude,
Thou madly-rushing multitude,
Loud as the tempest that o'er ocean raves!
Woe to the nations proud and strong,
That rush tumultuously along,
As rolls the foaming stream its long-resounding waves!
As the noise of mighty seas,
As the loudly-murmuring breeze,
Shall gath'ring nations rush, a pow'rful band:
Rise, God of Light, in burning wrath severe,
And stretch, to blast their proud career,
Thy arrow-darting hand!
Then shall their ranks to certain~fate be giv'n,
Then on their course Despair her fires shall cast,
Then shall they fly, to endless ruin driv'n,
As flies the thistle-down before the mountain-blast l

XVII
"Alas! in vain, in vain we call!
The stranger triumphs in our fall!

61

And Fate comes on, with ruthless frown,
To strike Palmyra's splendor down.
Urg'd by the steady breath of Time,
The desert-whirlwind sweeps sublime,
  The eddying sands in mountain-columns rise:
  Borne on the pinions of the gale,
  In one concenter'd cloud they sail;
    Along the darken'd skies.
It falls! it falls! on Thedmor's walls
The whelming weight of ruin falls
Th' avenging thunder-bolt is hurl'd,
Her pride is blotted from the world,
  Her name unknown in story:
The trav'ller on her site shall stand,
And seek, amid the desert-sand,
  The records of her glory!
Her palaces are crush'd, her tow'rs o'erthrown,
Oblivion follows stern, and marks her for his own!"

XVIII

How oft, the festal board around,
  These time-worn walls among,
Has rung the full symphonious sound
  Of rapture-breathing song!
Ah! little thought the wealthy proud,
When rosy pleasure laugh'd aloud,
That here, amid their ancient land,
  The wand'rer of the distant days
  Should mark, with sorrow-clouded gaze,
The mighty wilderness of sand;
While not a sound should meet his ear,
  Save of the desert-gales that sweep,
  In modulated murmurs deep,
    The wasted graves above,

Of those who once had revell'd here,
  In happiness and love!

XIX

Short is the space to man assign'd
  This earthly vale to tread
He wanders, erring, weak, and blind,
  By adverse passions led.
Love, the balm of ev'ry woe,
The dearest blessing man can know;
Jealousy, whose pois'nous breath
  Blasts affection's opining bud;
Stern Despair, that laughs in death;
  Black Revenge, that bathes in blood;
Fear, that his form in darkness shrouds,
  And trembles at the whisp'ring air;
And Hope, that pictures on the clouds
  Celestial visions, false, but fair;
    All rule by turns:
    To-day he burns
With ev'ry pang of keen distress;
    To-morrow's sky
    Bids sorrow fly
With dreams of promis'd happiness.

XX

From the earliest twilight-ray,
  That mark'd Creation's natal day,
    Till yesterday's declining fire,
  Thus still have roll'd, perplex'd by strife,
  The many-clashing wheels of life,
And still shall roll, till Time's last beams expire
And thus, in ev'ry age, in ev'ry clime,
  While circling years shall fly,

The varying deeds that mark the present time
Will be but shadows of the days gone by.

XXI

Along the desolated shore,
  Where, broad and swift, Euphrates flows,
The trav'ller's anxious eye can trace no more
  The spot where once the Queen of Cities rose.
Where old Persepolis sublimely tow'r'd,
    In cedar-groves embow'r'd,
  A rudely-splendid wreck alone remains,
The course of Fate no pomp or pow'r can shun
    Pollution tramples on thy giant-fanes,
      Oh City of the Sun!
Fall'n are the Tyrian domes of wealth and joy,
The hundred gates of Thebes, the tow'rs of Troy;
In shame and sorrow pre-ordain'd to cease,
Proud Salem met th' irrevocable doom;
In darkness sunk the arts and arms of Greece,
And the long glories of imperial Rome.

XXII

When the tyrants iron hand
The mountain-piles of Memphis rais'd,
That still the storms of angry Time defy,
  In self-adoring thought he gaz'd,
  And bade the massive labors stand,
    Till Nature's self should die!;
Presumptuous fool! the death-wind came,
And swept away thy worthless name;
And ages, with insidious flow,
Shall lay those blood-bought fabrics low.
Then shall the stranger pause, and oft be told,
"Here stood the mighty Pyramids of old!"

And smile, half-doubtful, when the tale he hears,
That speaks the wonders of the distant years

XXIII
Though Night awhile usurp the skies,
Yet soon the smiling Morn shall rise,
  And light and life restore;
Again the sun-beams gild the plain;
The youthful day returns again,
  But man returns no more.
  Though Winter's frown severe
  Deform the wasted year,
Spring smiles again, with renovated bloom;
  But what sweet Spring, with genial breath,
  Shall chase the icy sleep of death,
The dark and cheerless winter of the tomb ?
Hark! from the mansions of the dead,
What thrilling sounds of deepest import spread I
Sublimely mingled with the eddying gale,
Full on the desert-air these solemn accents sail:

XXIV
"Unthinking man! and cost thou weep,
  That clouds o'ercast thy little day?
That Death's stern hands so quickly sweep
  Thy ev'ry earthly hope away?
Thy rapid hours in darkness flow, '
  But well those rapid hours employ,
And they shall lead from realms of woe
  To realms of everlasting joy.
For though thy Father and thy God
Wave o'er thy head his chast'ning rod,
  Benignantly severe,
Yet future blessings shall repair,

In tenfold measure, ev'ry care,
  That marks thy progress here.

          XXV
"BOW THEN TO HIM, FOR HE IS GOOD,
  And loves the works His hands have made;
In earth, in air, in fire, in flood,
  His parent-bounty shines display'd.
BOW THEN TO HIM, FOR HE IS JUST,
  Though mortals scan His ways in vain;
Repine not, children of the dust!
  For HE in mercy sends ye pain.
BOW THEN TO HIM, FOR HE IS GREAT,
And was, ere NATURE, TIME, and FATE,
  Began their mystic flight;
And still shall be, when consummating flame
  Shall plunge this universal frame
    In everlasting night.
BOW THEN TO HIM, the LORD of ALL.
Whose nod bids empires rise and fall,
  EARTH, HEAV'N, and NATURE's SIRE;
To HIM, Who, matchless and alone,
Has fix'd in boundless space His throne,
Unchang'd, unchanging still,while worlds and suns expire!"

PALMYRA

(2ND EDITION)

---*anankta ton pantôn huperbal-
lonta chronon makarôn.*
Pind[ar. *Hymn.* frag. 33].

ANALYSIS

An address to the spirit of ancient times introduces an evening contemplation on the ruined magnificence of Palmyra, on the obscurity that involves its history, its monuments, its inscriptions in a language now unknown. 'Fancy calls up the forms of its monarchs, chiefs, and philosophers; few of whose names, in addition to those of odenathus, Zenobia, and Longinus, have survived the lapse of years. Time asserts his empire over the ruins, and dissipates the phantoms of fancy. The silence and solitude of the evening twilight, in these scenes of desolated splendor, present an impressive contrast to the days of their past prosperity. Human passions, and the actions that result from them, are nearly the same in all ages and nations. All the works of man are subject to the same decay. Even these ruins will disappear from the desert. Time and change have absolute dominion over every thing terrestrial but virtue and the mind.

67

PALMYRA

Spirit of the days of yore!
   Thou! who, in thy haunted cave,
By the torrent's sounding shore,
   Mark'st the autumnal tempest rave:
Or, where on some ivied wall
Twilight-mingled moonbeams fall,
Deep in aisles and cloisters dim,
Hear'st the grey monks' verpser hymn:
Or, beneath the cypress shade,
Where forgotten chiefs are laid,
Pacing slow with solemn tread,
Breathest the verse that wakes the dead---
By the ivied convent lone,
By the Runic warrior's stone,
By the mountain-cataract's roar,
Spirit! thee I seek no more.
Let me, remote from earthly care,
Thy philosophic vigils share,
Amid the wrecks of ancient time,
More sad, more solemn, more sublime,
Where, half-sunk in seas of sand,
Thedmor's marble wastes expand.

These silent wrecks, more eloquent than speech,
   Full many a tale of awful note impart:
Truths more severe than bard or sage can teach
   This pomp of ruin presses on the heart
Sad through the palm the evening breezes-sigh:
   No sound of man the solitude pervades,
Where shattered forms of ancient monarchs lie,
   Mid grass-grown halls, and falling colonnades.

Beneath the drifting sand, the clustering weed,
  Rest the proud relics of departed power.
None may the trophy-cinctured tablet read,
  On votive urn, or monumental tower,
Nor tell whose wasted forms the mouldering tombs
embower.

    Enthusiast fancy, robed in light,
    Dispels oblivion's deepening night.
    Her charms a solemn train unfold,
    Sublime on evening clouds of gold,
    Of sceptred kings, in proud array,
    And laurelled chiefs, and sages grey.
    But whose the forms, oh fame! declare,
    That crowd majestic on the air?
    Pour from thy deathless roll the praise
    Of kings renowned in elder days.
    I call in vain! The welcome strain
      Of praise to them no more shall sound:
    Their actions bright must sleep in night,
      Till time shall cease his mystic round.
    The glories of their ancient sway
    The stream of years has swept away:
    Their names, that nations heard with fear,
    Shall ring no more on mortal ear.
    Yet still the muse's eye may trace
    The noblest chief of Thedmor's race,
    Who, by Euphrates' startling waves,
Bade outraged Rome her prostrate might unfold,
    Tore from the brow of Persia's pride
    The wreath in crimson victory dyed,
      And o'er his flying slaves
      Tumultuous ruin rolled.
    Throned by his side, a lovely form,

In youthful majesty sublime,
Like sun-beams through the scattering storm,
Shines through the floating mists of time:
Even as in other years she shone,
When here she fixed her desert-throne,
Triumphant in the transient smiles of fate;
When Zabdas led her conquering bands
O'er Asia's many-peopled lands,
And subject monarchs thronged her palace-gate:
Ere yet stern war's avenging storm,
Captivity's dejected form,
And death, in solitude and darkness furled,
Closed round the setting star, that ruled the eastern world.

Dim shades around her move again,
From memory blotted by the lapse of years:
Yet, foremost in the sacred train,
The venerable sage appears,
Who once, these desolate arcades
And time-worn porticoes among,
Disclosed to princely youths and high-born maids
The secret fountains of Mæonian song,
And traced the mazy warblings of the lyre,
With all a critic's art, and all a poet's fire.

What mystic form, uncouth and dread,
With withered cheek, and hoary head,
Swift as the death-fire cleaves the sky,
Swept on sounding pinions by?
'Twas Time. I know the foe of kings,
His scythe, and sand, and eagle-wings:
He cast a burning look around,
And waved his bony hand, and frowned.

Far from the spectre's scowl of fire,
Fancy's feeble forms retire:
Her air-born phantoms melt away,
Like stars before the rising day.

One shadowy tint enwraps the plain:
    No form is near, no steps intrude,
To break the melancholy reign
    Of silence and of solitude.
Ah! little thought the wealthy proud,
When rosy pleasure laughed aloud,
And music, with symphonious swell,
Attuned to joy her festal shell,
That here, amid their ancient land,
    The wanderer of the distant days
    Should mark, with sorrow-clouded gaze,
The mighty wilderness of sand,
While not a sound should meet his ear,
    Save of the desert-gales, that sweep,
    In modulated murmurs deep,
    The wasted graves above
Of those, who once had revelled here
    In happiness and love.

Short is the space to man assigned,
    His earthly vale to tread.
He wanders, erring, weak, and blind,
    By adverse passions led:
Love, that with feeling's tenderest flow
To rapture turns divided woe,
And brightens every smile of fate
That kindred souls participate:
Jealousy, whose poisonous breath

71

Blasts affection's opening bud:
Wild despair, that laughs in death:
  Stern revenge, that bathes in blood:
Fear, that his form in darkness shrouds,
  And trembles at the whispering air:
And hope, that pictures on the clouds
  Celestial visions, false, but fair.

From the earliest twilight-ray,
That marked creation's natal day,
  Till yesterday's declining fire,
Thus still have rolled, perplexed by strife,
  he many-mingling wheels of life,
And still shall roll, till time's last beams expire.
And thus, in every age, in every clime,
  While years swift-circling fly,
The varying deeds, that mark the present time,
Will be but shadows of the days gone by.

Swift as the meteor's midnight course,
Swift as the cataract's headlong force,
Swift as the clouds, whose changeful forms
Hang on the rear of flying storms,
So swift is Time's colossal stride
Above the wrecks of human pride.
These temples, awful in decay,
  Whose ancient splendor half endures,
These arches, dim in parting day,
  These dust-defiled entablatures,
These shafts, whose prostrate pride around
  The desert-weed entwines its wreath,
These capitals, that strew the ground,
  Their shattered colonnades beneath,

These pillars, white in lengthening files,
Grey tombs, and broken peristyles,
May yet, through many an age, retain
The pomp of Thedmor's wasted reign:
But Time still shakes, with giant-tread,
The marble city of the dead,
That crushed at last, a shapeless heap,
Beneath the drifted sands shall sleep.

The flower, that drinks the morning-dew,
    Far on the evening gale shall fly:
The bark, that glides o'er ocean blue,
    Dashed on the distant rocks shall lie:
The tower, that frowns in martial pride,
    Shall by the lightning-brand be riven:
The arch, that spans the summer tide,
    Shall down the wintry floods be driven:
The tomb, that guards the great one's name,
    Shall yield to time its sacred trust:
The laurel of imperial fame
    Shall wither in unwatered dust.
His mantle dark oblivion flings
Around the monuments of kings,
Who once to conquest shouting myriads bore.
Fame's trumpet-blast, and victory's clarion shrill,
    Pass, like an echo of the hill,
That breathes one wild response, and then is heard no more.

But ne'er shall earthly time throw down
    The immortal pile that virtue rears:
Her golden throne, and starry crown,
    Decay not with revolving years:
For He, whose solemn voice controlled

Necessity's mysterious sway,
And yon vast orbs from chaos rolled
Along the elliptic paths of day,
Has fixed her empire, vast and high,
Where primogenial harmony
Unites, in ever-cloudless skies,
Affection's death-divided ties;
Where wisdom, with unwearying gaze,
The universal scheme surveys,
And truth, in central light enshrined,
Leads to its source sublime the indissoluble mind.

BEYOND THE SEA

FROM CROTCHET CASTLE

BEYOND the sea, beyond the sea,
My heart is gone, far, far from me;
And ever on its track will flee
My thoughts, my dreams, beyond the sea.

Beyond the sea, beyond the sea,
The swallow wanders fast and free:
Oh, happy bird! were I like thee,
I, too, would fly beyond the sea.

Beyond the sea, beyond the sea,
Are kindly hearts and social glee:
But here for me they may not be;
My heart is gone beyond the sea.

A BILL FOR THE BETTER PROMOTION OF OPPRESSION ON THE SABBATH DAY

FORASMUCH as the Canter's and Fanatic's Lord
Sayeth peace and joy are by me abhorred;
And would fill each Sunday with gloom and pain
For all too poor his regard to obtain;
And forasmuch as the laws heretofore
Have not sufficiently squeezed the poor
Be it therefore enacted by Commons, King
And Lords, a crime for any thing
To be done on the Sabbath by any rank
Excepting the rich. No beer may be drank,
Food eaten, rest taken, away from home,
And each House shall a Sunday prison become;
And spies and jailers must carefully see,
Under severest penaly,
None stirs but to conventicle,
Thrice a day at toll of bell.
And each sickly cit who dare engage
His place by steamer, fly or stage,
With owner thereof shall by this said bill,
Be punished with fine, imprisonment or treadmill.
But nothing herein is designed to discourage
Priest, noble or squire from the use of his carriage.
No ship shall move however it blow,
The Devil a bit shall said ship go
Whether the winds will let it or no;
And, as winds and weather we cannot imprison,
Owners, Captain and sailors we therefore shall seize on,

And whereas oxen, lambs and sheep
About the roads and lanes will creep,
And cocks and hens and ducks and geese
Will not on Sunday hold their peace,
Be it enacted that foresaid beasts,
If not belonging to gentry or priests,
Be caught and whipped and pounded on Sunday,
And sold to pay expences on Monday.
The drunkard, who paid five shillings before,
Shall now pay twenty shillings more,
And mine host, if on Sabbath he dare unloose
A bolt, shall be fined and his licence lose.
All oranges, cakes & lollypop
Shall be sized; & every open shop
Shall be fined a pound an hour till it stop.
Till nine the milkman may ply his trade,
For pious breakfasts must be made
At he risk of his soul. And the bakers at last,
When the poor man's dinner is clearly past,
Must set to work, the godly scorning
Stale rolls and bread on a Monday morning.
That Justices may have less to do,
'Tis enacted they may convict on view,
And shall, if they think the couse more drastic
Transfer to Courts Ecclesiastic.
All informers shall pass scot free,
However false their averments may be;
And witnesses who have no mind
To convict shall be imprisoned and fined.
And whereas from this act's operation
Are exempted the following ranks in this nation:
The rich man's servants---they cannot be spared
(In spite of Scripture) from working hard---;
Milkmen in the morning; at evening the bakers,
With constables, doctors, thieves, parsons, tollmakers;

77

And parties for music, gambling or dinners
Are hereby exempt, when the rich are the sinners;
For no party whatever has aught to fear
From said act who has more than £500 a year.

CASTLES IN THE AIR

MY thoughts by night are often filled
  With visions false as fair:
For in the past alone I build
  My castles in the air.

I dwell not now on what may be:
  Night shadows o'er the scene:
But still my fancy wanders free
  Through that which might have been.

DUET

FROM THE THREE DOCTORS

Milestone: ALL my troubles disappear,
   When the dinner-bell I hear,
   Over woodland, dale, and fell,
   Swinging slow with solemn swell,---
     The dinner-bell! the dinner-bell!

Hippy: What can bid my heart-ache fly?
   What can bid my heart-ache die?
   What can all the ills dispel,
   In my morbid frame that dwell?
     The dinner-bell! the dinner-bell!

Both: Hark!---along the tangled ground,
   Loudly floats the pleasing sound!
   Sportive Fauns to Dryads tell,
   'Tis the cheerful dinner-bell!
     The dinner-bell! the dinner-bell!

A FRAGMENT

NAY, deem me not insensible, Cesario,
To female charms; nor think this heart of mine
Is cas'd in adamant; because, forsooth,
I cannot ogle, and hyperbolize,
And whisper tender nothings in the ear
Of ev'ry would-be beauty, holding out
The bright but treacherous flame of flattery,
To watch the she-moths of a drawing room
Sport round the beam, and burn their pretty wings,
Ere conscious of their danger: yet, believe me,
I love a maid whose untranscended form
Is yet less lovely than her spotless mind.
With modest frankness, unaffected genius,
Unchang'd good humour, beauty void of art,
And polish'd wit that seeks not to offend,
And winning smiles that seek not to betray,
She charms the sight, and fascinates the soul.
Where dwells this matchless nymph? alas, Cesario,
'Tis but a sickly creature of my fancy,
Unparallel'd in nature.

A GLEE

QUICKLY pass the social glass,
   Hence with idle sorrow!
No delay---enjoy today,
   Think not of tomorrow!
Life at best is but a span,
Let us taste it whilst we can;
Let us still with smiles confess,
All our aim is happiness!

Childish fears, and sighs and tears
   Still to us are strangers;
Why destroy the bud of joy
   With ideal dangers?
Let the song of pleasure swell;
Care with us shall never dwell;
Let us still with smiles confess,
All our aim is happiness!

I DUG, BENEATH A CYPRESS SHADE

I DUG, beneath a cypress shade,
  What well might seem an elfin's grave;
And every pledge in earth I laid,
  That erst thy false affection gave.

I press'd them down the sod beneath;
  I placed one mossy stone above;
And twined the rose's fading wreath
  Around the sepulchre of love.

Frail as thy love, the flowers were dead
  Ere yet the evening sun was set:
But years shall see the cypress spread,
  Immutable as my regret.

INSTEAD OF SITTING
WRAPPED UP IN FLANNEL

———————————

INSTEAD of sitting wrapped up in flannel
   With rheumatism in every joint,
I wish I was in the English Channel,
   Just going 'round the Lizard Point
All southward bound, with the seas before me,
   I should not care whether smooth or rough,
For then no visitors would call to bore me,
   Of whose 'good-mornings' I have had enough.

LIFE'S UNCERTAIN DAY

THE briefest part of life's uncertain day,
Youth's lovely blossom, hastes to swift decay:
While love, wine, song, enhance our gayest mood
Old age creeps on, nor thought, nor understood.

LINES ON THE DEATH OF JULIA

ACCEPT, bright spirit, reft in life's best bloom
This votive wreath to thy untimely tomb.
Formed to adorn all scenes, and charm in all,
The fire-side circle, and the courtly hall;
Thy friends to gladden, and thy home to bless;---
Fair form thou hadst, and grace, and graciousness;
A mind that sought, a tongue that spoke, the truth,
And thought mature beneath the smiles of youth.
Dear, dear young friend! ingenuous, cordial heart!
And can it be, that thou shouldst first depart?
That age should sorrow o'er thy youthful shrine?
It owns more near, more sacred griefs than mine;
Yet, midst the many who thy loss deplore,
Few loved thee better, and few mourn thee more.

LOVE AND AGE

FROM GRYLL GRANGE

I PLAY'D with you 'mid cowslips blowing,
   When I was six and you were four;
When garlands weaving, flower-balls throwing,
   Were pleasures soon to please no more.
Through groves and meads, o'er grass and heather,
   With little playmates, to and fro,
We wander'd hand in hand together;
   But that was sixty years ago.

You grew a lovely roseate maiden,
   And still our early love was strong;
Still with no care our days were laden,
   They glided joyously along;
And I did love you very dearly,
   How dearly words want power to show;
I thought your heart was touch'd as nearly;
   But that was fifty years ago.

Then other lovers came around you,
   Your beauty grew from year to year,
And many a splendid circle found you
   The centre of its glimmering sphere.
I saw you then, first vows forsaking,
   On rank and wealth your hand bestow;

O, then I thought my heart was breaking!--
  But that was forty years ago.

And I lived on, to wed another:
  No cause she gave me to repine;
And when I heard you were a mother,
  I did not wish the children mine.
My own young flock, in fair progression,
  Made up a pleasant Christmas row:
My joy in them was past expression;
  But that was thirty years ago.

You grew a matron plump and comely,
  You dwelt in fashion's brightest blaze;
My earthly lot was far more homely;
  But I too had my festal days.
No merrier eyes have ever glisten'd
  Around the hearth-stone's wintry glow,
Than when my youngest child was christen'd;
  But that was twenty years ago.

Time pass'd. My eldest girl was married,
  And I am now a grandsire gray;
One pet of four years old I've carried
  Among the wild-flower'd meads to play.
In our old fields of childish pleasure,
  Where now, as then, the cowslips blow,
She fills her basket's ample measure;
  And that is not ten years ago.

But though first love's impassion'd blindness
  Has pass'd away in colder light,
I still have thought of you with kindness,
  And shall do, till our last good-night.
The ever-rolling silent hours

Will bring a time we shall not know,
When our young days of gathering flowers
Will be an hundred years ago.

MARGARET LOVE PEACOCK

AN EPITAPH

LONG night succeeds thy little day;
 Oh blighted blossom! can it be,
That this grey stone, and grassy clay,
 Have clos'd our anxious care of thee?

The half-form'd speech of artless thought
 That spoke a mind beyond thy years;
The song, the dance, by nature taught;
 The sunny smiles, the transient tears;

The symmetry of face and form,
 The eye with light and life replete;
The little heart so fondly warm,
 The voice so musically sweet;

These, lost to hope, in memory yet
 Around the hearts that lov'd thee cling,
Shadowing, with long and vain regret,
 The too fair promise of thy spring.

NEWARK ABBEY

AUGUST, 1842
WITH A REMEMBRANCE OF AUGUST, 1807

I GAZE, where August's sunbeam falls
Along these grey and lonely walls,
Till in its light absorbed appears
The lapse of five-and-thirty years.

If change there be, I trace it not
In all this consecrated spot:
No new imprint of Ruin's march
On roofless wall and frameless arch:
The hilss, the woods, the fields, the stream,
Are basking in the self-same beam:
The fall, that turns the unseen mill
As then it murmured, murmurs still:
It seems, as if in one were cast
The present and the imaged past,
Spanning, as with bridge sublime,
That awful lapse of human time,
That gulph, unfathomably spread
Between the living and the dead.

For all too well my spirit feels
The only change this place reveals:
The sunbeams play, the breezes stir,
Unseen, unfelt, unheard by her,

91

Who, on that long-past August day,
First saw with me those ruins grey.

    Whatever span the fates allow,
Ere I shall be as she is now,
Still in my bosom's inmost cell
Shall that deep-treasured memory dwell:
That, more than language can express,
Pure miracle of loveliness,
Whose voice so sweet, whose eyes so bright,
Were my soul's music, and its light,
In those blest days, when life was new,
And hope was false, but love was true.

RICH & POOR;
OR SAINT & SINNER

THE poor man's sins are glaring;
In the face of ghostly warning
   He is caught in the fact
   Of an overt act---
Buying greens on a Sunday morning.

The rich man's sins are hidden
In the pomp of wealth and station;
   And escape the sight
   Of the children of light,
Who are wise in their generation.

The rich man has a kitchen,
And cooks to dress his dinner;
   The poor who would roast
   To the baker's must post,
And thus becomes a sinner.

The rich man has a cellar,
And a ready butler by him;
   The poor man must steer
   For his pint of beer
Where the saint can't choose but to spy him.

The rich man's painted windows
Hide the concerts of the quality;
   The poor can but share
    A crack'd fiddle in the air,
Which offends all sound morality.

The rich man is invisible
In the crowd of his gay society;
   But the poor man's delight
    Is a sore in the sight,
And a stench in the nose of piety.

THERE IS A FEVER OF THE SPIRIT

FROM NIGHTMARE ABBEY

THERE is a fever of the spirit,
The brand of Cain's unresting doom,
Which in the lone dark souls that bear it
Glows like the lamp in Tullia's tomb:

Unlike that lamp, its subtle fire
Burns, blasts, consumes its cell, the heart,
Till, one by one, hope, joy, desire,
Like dreams of shadowy smoke depart.

When hope, love, life itself, are only
Dust--spectral memories--dead and cold--
The unfed fire burns bright and lonely,
Like that undying lamp of old:

And by that drear illumination,
Till time its clay-built home has rent,
Thought broods on feeling's desolation
The soul is its own monument.

SIR HORNBOOK

OR CHILDE LAUNCELOT'S EXPEDITION

A GRAMMATICO-ALLEGORICAL BALLAD

I.

O'er bush and briar Childe Launcelot sprung [1]
    With ardent hopes elate,
And loudly blew the horn that hung
    Before Sir Hornbook's gate.

The inner portals opened wide,
    And forward strode the chief,
Arrayed in paper helmet's pride,
    And arms of golden leaf.

--"What means,"--he cried,--"This daring noise,
    That wakes the summer day?
I hate all idle truant boys:
    Away, Sir Childe, away!"--

--"No idle, truant boy am I,"--
    Childe Launcelot answered straight;

--"Resolved to climb this hill so high,
    I seek thy castle gate.

"Behold the talisman I bear,
    And aid my bold design:"--
Sir Hornbook gazed, and written there,
    Knew Emulation's sign

"If Emulation sent thee here,"
    Sir Hornbook quick replied,
"My merrymen all shall soon appear,
To aid thy cause with shield and spear,
And I will head thy bold career,
    And prove thy faithful guide."--

Loud rung the chains; the drawbridge fell;
    The gates asunder flew:
The knight thrice beat the portal bell,
    And thrice he call'd "Halloo."

And out, and out, in hasty rout,
    By ones, twos, threes, and fours;
His merrymen rush'd the walls without,
    And stood before the doors.

II.

Full six and twenty men were they, [2]
    In line of battle spread:

The first that came was mighty A,
    The last was little Z.

Six Vocal men Sir Hornbook had, [3]
    Four Double men to boot, [4]
And four were Liquids soft and sad, [5]
    And all the rest were Mute. [6]

He called his *Corporal*, Syllable, [7]
    To range the scatter'd throng;
And *Captain* Word dispos'd them well [8]
    In bands compact and strong.

--"Now mark, Sir Childe,"--Sir Hornbook said:--
    "These well-compacted powers,
Shall lead thy vent'rous steps to tread
    Through all the Muses' bowers,

"If rightly thou thyself address,
    To use their proffer'd aid:
Still unallur'd by idleness,
    By labor undismay'd;

"For many troubles intervene,
    And perils widely spread,
Around the groves of evergreen,
    That crown this mountain's head:
But rich reward he finds, I ween,
    Who through them all has sped."--

Childe Launcelot felt his bosom glow
    At thought of noble deed;

Resolved through every path to go,
  Where that bold knight should lead.

Sir Hornbook wound his bugle horn,
  Full long, and loud, and shrill;
His merrymen all, for conquest born,
With armour glittering to the morn,
  Went marching up the hill.

III.

--"What men are you beside the way?"--
  The bold Sir Hornbook cried:
--"My name is *The*, my brother's *A*,"--
  Sir Article replied. [9]

"My brother's home is any where, [10]
  At large and undefin'd;
But I a preference ever bear [11]
For one fix'd spot, and settle there;
  Which speaks my constant mind."

--"What ho! Childe Launcelot! seize them there,
  And look you have them sure!"--
--Sir Hornbook cried,--"my men shall bear
  Your captives off secure."--

The twain were seized: Sir Hornbook blew
  His bugle loud and shrill:

His merrymen all, so stout and true,
Went marching up the hill.

IV.

And now a wider space they gained,
  A steeper, harder ground,
Where by one ample wall contained,
  All earthly *things* they found: [12]

All *beings*, rich, poor, weak, or wise,
  Were there, full strange to see,
And *attributes* and *qualities*
  Of high and low degree.

Before the circle stood a knight,
  Sir Substantive his name, [13]
With Adjective, his lady bright,
  Who *seemed* a portly dame;

Yet only *seemed*; for whenso'er
  She strove to *stand alone*, [14]
She proved no more than smoke and air,
  Who looked like flesh and bone.

And therefore to her husband's arm
  She clung for evermore,
And lent him many a grace and charm
  He had not known before;

Yet these the knight felt well advised,
   He might have done without;
For lightly foreign help he prized
   He was so staunch and stout.

Five sons had they, their dear delight,
   Of different forms and faces;
And *two* of them were Numbers bright, [15]
   And *three* they christened Cases. [16]

Now loudly rung Sir Hornbook's horn;
   Childe Launcelot poised his spear;
And on they rushed, to conquest borne,
   In swift and full career.

Sir Substantive kicked down the wall:
   It fell with furious rattle:
And earthly *things* and *beings* all
   Rushed forth to join the battle.

But earthly *things* and *beings* all,
   Through mixed in boundless plenty,
Must one by one dissolving fall
   To Hornbook's six-and-twenty.

Childe Launcelot won the arduous fray,
   And, when they ceased from strife,
Led stout Sir Substantive away,
   His children, and his wife.

Sir Hornbook wound his horn again,
   Full long, and loud, and shrill:

His merrymen all, a warlike train,
    Went marching up the hill.

V.

Now when Sir Pronoun look'd abroad, [17]
    And spied the coming train,
He left his fort beside the road,
    And ran with might and main.

Two cloth-yard shafts from I and U,
    Went forth with whizzing sound:
Like lightning sped the arrows true;
    Sir Pronoun pressed the ground:
But darts of science ever flew
    To conquer, not to wound.

His fear was great: his hurt was small:
    Childe Launcelot took his hand:
--"Sir Knight,"--said he,--"though doomed to fall
    Before my conquering band,

"Yet knightly treatment shall you find,
    On faith of cavalier:
Then join Sir Substantive behind,
    And follow our career."--

Sir Substantive, that man of might,
    Felt knightly anger rise;

For he had marked Sir Pronoun's flight
  With no approving eyes.

"Great Substantive, my sovereign liege!"--
  Thus sad Sir Pronoun cried,
--"When you had fallen in furious siege,
  Could I the shock abide?"

"That all resistance would be vain,
  Too well, alas! I knew:
For what could I, when you were ta'en,
  Your poor *lieutenant*, do?"

Then louder rung Sir Hornbook's horn,
  In signals long and shrill:
His merrymen all, for conquest born,
  Went marching up the hill.

VI.

Now steeper grew the rising ground,
  And rougher grew the road,
As up the steep ascent they wound
  To bold Sir Verb's abode. [18]

Sir Verb was old, and many a year,
  All scenes and climates seeing,
Had run a wild and strange career
  Through every mode of being.

And every aspect, shape, and change
    Of *action*, and of *passion*:
And known to him was all the range
    Of feeling, taste, and fashion.

He was an Augur, quite at home
    In all things present done, [19]
Deeds past, and every act to come
    In ages yet to run.

Entrenched in intricacies strong,
    Ditch, fort, and palisado,
He marked with scorn the coming throng,
    And breathed a bold bravado:

--"Ho! who are you that dare invade
    My turrets, moats, and fences?
Soon will your vaunting courage fade,
When you on the walls, in lines array'd,
You see me marshal undismay'd
    My host of moods and tenses."--[20]

--"In vain,"--Childe Launcelot cried in scorn,--
    --"On them is your reliance;"--
Sir Hornbook wound his bugle horn,
    And twange'd a loud defiance.

They swam the moat, they scal'd the wall,
    Sir Verb, with rage and shame,
Beheld his valiant *general* fall,
    Infinitive by name.[21]

Indicative *declar'd* the foes [22]
    Should perish by his hand;
And stout Imperative arose, [23]
    The squadron to *command.*

Potential and Subjunctive [24] then
    Came forth with *doubt* and *chance*: [25]
All fell alike, with all their men,
    Before Sir Hornbook's lance.

Action and Passion nought could do
    To save Sir Verb from fate;
Whose doom poor Participle knew, [26]
    He must *participate.*

Then Adverb, who had skulk'd behind, [27]
    To shun the mighty jar,
Came forward, and himself resign'd
    A prisoner of war.

Three children of Imperative,
    Full strong, though somewhat small,
Next forward came, themselves to give
    To conquering Launcelot's thrall.

Conjunction press'd to join the crowd; [28]
    But Preposition swore, [29]
Though Interjection sobb'd aloud, [30]
    That he would *go before.*

Again his horn Sir Hornbook blew,
    Full long, and loud, and shrill;

His merrymen all, so stout and true,
    Went marching up the hill.

VII.

Sir Syntax dwelt in thick fir-grove, [31]
    All strown with scraps of flowers, [32]
Which he had pluck'd to please his love,
    Among the Muses' bowers.

His love was gentle Prosody,
    More fair than morning beam;
Who liv'd beneath a flowering tree,
    Beside a falling stream.

And these two claim'd, with high pretence
    The whole Parnassian ground,
Albeit some little difference
    Between their taste was found:
Sir Syntax he was all for sense,
    And Prosody for sound.

Yet in them both the Muses fair
    Exceedingly delighted;
And thought no earthly thing so rare,
That might with that fond twain compare,
    When they were both *united*.

--"Ho! yield, Sir Syntax!"--Hornbook cried,
    "This youth must pass thy grove,
Led on by me, his faithful guide,
    In yonder bowers to rove."--

Thereat full much, Sir Syntax said,
  But found resistance vain:
And through his grove Childe Launcelot sped,
  With all Sir Hornbook's train.

They reach'd the tree where Prosody
  Was singing in the shade:
Great joy Childe Launcelot had to see,
  And hear that lovely maid.

Now, onward as they press'd along,
  Did nought their course oppose;
Till full before the martial throng
  The Muses' gates arose.

There Etymology they found,
  Who scorn'd surrounding fruits;
And ever dug in deepest ground,
  For old and mouldy Roots.

Sir Hornbook took Childe Launcelot's hand,
  And tears at parting fell:
--"Sir Childe,"--he said,--"with all my band
  I bid you here farewell.

"Then wander through these sacred bowers,
  Unfearing and alone:
All shrubs are hear, and fruits, and flowers,
  To happiest climates known."--

Once more his horn Sir Hornbook blew,
  A parting signal shrill:
His merrymen all, so stout and true,
  Went marching down the hill.

Childe Launcelot pressed the sacred ground,
   With hope's exulting glow;
Some future song perchance may sound
The wondrous thing which there he found,
   If you the same would know.

FOOTNOTES

1 Childe, in our old ballads, often signifies a knight.

2 There are twenty-six letters, A. B. C. D. E. F. G. H. I. J. K. L. M. N. O. P. Q. R. S. T. U. V. W. X. Y. Z.

3. Of these are vowels, a. e. i. o. u. y.

4 Four are double letters j. w. x. z.

5 Four are liquids, k. m. n. r.

6 And twelve are mutes, b. c. d. f. g. h. k. p. p. s. t. v.

7 A syllable is a distinct sound of one or more letters pronounced in a breath.

8 Words are articulate sounds used by common consent, as signs of our ideas.

9 There are two articles, the, definite; a or an, indefinite.

10 The indefinite article is used generally and indeterminately to point out one single thing of a kind: as, "There is a dog;" "Give me an orange."

11 The definite article defines and specifies particular objects: as, "Those are the men;"--"Give me the book."

12 A noun is the name of whatsoever thing or being we see or discourse of.

13 Nouns are of two kinds, substantives and adjectives. A noun substantive declares its own meaning, and requires not another world to be joined with it to show its signification; as, man, book, apple.

14 A noun adjective cannot stand alone, but always requires to be joined with a substantive, of which it shows the nature or quality, as, "a good girl,"--"a naughty boy."

15 Nouns have two numbers, singular and plural;--

16 and three cases: nominative, possessive, and objective.

17 A pronoun is used instead of a noun, and may be considered its locum tenens, or deputy: as, "The King is gone to Windsor, he will return to-morrow."

18 A verb is a word which signifies to be, to do, or to suffer; as, "I am, I love, I am loved."

19 The two lines in Italics are taken from Chapman's Homer.

20 Verbs have five moods: The indicative, imperative, potential, subjunctive, and infinitive.

21 The infinitive mood expresses a thing in a general and unlimited manner: as, "To love, to walk, to be ruled."

22 The indicative mood simply indicates or declares a thing: as, "He loves:" "he is loved:" or asks a question: as, "Does he love?"--"Is he loved?"

23 The imperative mood commands or entreats: as, "Depart:" "Come hither:"--"Forgive me."

24 The potential mood implies possiblity or obligation: as, "It may rain:"--"They shouldlearn."

25 The subjunctive mood implies contingency: as, "if he were good, he would be happy."

26 The participle is a certain form of the verb, and is so called from participating the nature of a verb and an adjective: as, "he is an admired charcter; she is a loving child."

27 The adverb is joined to verbs, to adjectives, and to other adverbs, to qualify their signification: as, "that is a remarkably swift horse: it is extremely well done."

28 A conjunction is a part of speech chiefly used to connect words: as, "King and constitution;" or sentences: as, "I went to the theater, and saw the new pantomime."

29 A preposition is most commonly set before another word to show its relation to some word or sentence preceding: as, "The fisherman went down the river with his boat."

Conjunctions and Prepositions are for the most part Imperative moods of obsolete verbs: Thus, and signifies add: "John and Peter--John add peter:"--"The fisherman with his boat--The fisherman, join his boat."

30 Interjections are words thrown in between the parts of sentence, to express passions or emotions: as "Oh! Alas!"

31 Syntax is that part of grammar, which treats of the agreement and construction of words in a sentence.

32 I allude to the poetical fragments with which syntax is illustrated.

[*Sir Hornbook* was first published in 1814]

* 9 7 8 1 5 2 8 7 0 4 3 6 6 *